ANIMAL CLASSIFICATION

REPTILES

by
Steffi Cavell-Clarke

KidHaven PUBLISHING

Published in 2017 by
KidHaven Publishing, an Imprint of Greenhaven Publishing, LLC
353 3rd Avenue
Suite 255
New York, NY 10010

Designer: Drue Rintoul
Editor: Grace Jones

Cataloging-in-Publication Data

Names: Cavell-Clarke, Steffi.
Title: Reptiles / Steffi Cavell-Clarke.
Description: New York : KidHaven Publishing, 2017. | Series: Animal classification | Includes index.
Identifiers: ISBN 9781534520219 (pbk.) | ISBN 9781534520233 (library bound) | ISBN
9781534520226 (6 pack) | ISBN 9781534520240 (ebook)
Subjects: LCSH: Reptiles–Juvenile literature.
Classification: LCC QL644.2 C38 2017 | DDC 597.9–dc23

Printed in the United States of America

CPSIA compliance information: Batch #CW17KL: For further information contact Greenhaven Publishing LLC, New York, New York at 1-844-317-7404.

Please visit our website, www.greenhavenpublishing.com. For a free color catalog of all our
high-quality books, call toll free 1-844-317-7404 or fax 1-844-317-7405.

Photo Credits
Abbreviations: l-left, r-right, b-bottom, t-top, c-center, m-middle.

Front Cover – Fedor Selivanov. Back Cover – domnitsky. 4l – Marques. 4b – Philip Evans. 5 – Rich Carey. 6 – Christopher Mansfield.
7tl – Business stock. 7tr – Brandon Alms. 8tl – Eric Isselee. 8bl – Andrew Burgess. 8tr – Eric Isselee. 8br – Rudmer Zwerver.
9 – Mark52. 10 – Eric Isselee. 11 – alexilena. 12ml – Aleksey Stemmer. 12br – Lana Langlois. 12bl – Tungphoto. 13 – tropicdreams.
14 – Kuttelvaserova Stuchelova. 15t – underworld. 15b – Michiel de Wit. 16bl – Vladimir Wrangel. 16br – okanakdeniz.
17 – nattanan726. 18 – Cathy Keifer. 19 – EpicStockMedia. 20t – Matt Jeppson. 20b – ANDRZEJ GRZEGORCZYK. 21 – cellistka.
22t – Heiko Kiera. 22b – Paul Tessier. 23t – Joyce Mar. 23b – Heiko Kiera. 24 – cellistka. 25 – Lidiya Oleandra. 26 – Eric Isselee.
27 – Ryan M. Bolton. 28 – KRISS75. 29 – Fotos593. Images are courtesy of Shutterstock.com, unless stated otherwise. With thanks to
Getty Images, Thinkstock Photo, and iStockphoto.

CONTENTS

Words that are underlined are explained in the glossary on page 31.

THE ANIMAL KINGDOM

The animal kingdom includes more than 8 million known living <u>species</u>. They come in many different shapes and sizes, they each do weird and wonderful things, and they live all over Earth.

From the freezing Arctic waters to the hottest desert in the world, animals have <u>adapted</u> to often extreme and diverse conditions on Earth.

Even though each and every animal species is <u>unique</u>, they still share certain characteristics with each other. These shared characteristics are used to classify animals. There are six main groups used to classify animals. They are mammals, reptiles, birds, insects, amphibians, and fish.

This turtle is a reptile.

10,000 **new** species of animals are discovered **every year.**

REPTILES

WHAT IS A REPTILE?

Reptiles have backbones, and their skin is almost completely covered in scales. Most reptiles lay soft-shelled eggs on land.

Reptiles generally live on land, but some, such as turtles and crocodiles, can also live in water. Reptiles are cold-blooded animals, which means their body temperature changes depending on the temperature of their environment.

Great Lakes bush vipers can be found near water in Africa.

6

There are more than 9,000 different species of reptiles in the world today. Many species look different from one another and have their own individual features that help them survive in their habitats. Snakes, lizards, crocodiles, and tortoises are all types of reptiles.

saltwater crocodile

leaf chameleon

The largest reptile on Earth is the saltwater crocodile, which can grow up to 19.7 feet (6 m) long, while the leaf chameleon is one of the smallest reptiles on Earth, measuring around 1.2 inches (3 cm) long.

REPTILE CHECKLIST

- generally lays eggs
- breathes using lungs
- has scales
- is cold-blooded
- is a <u>vertebrate</u>

BODY PARTS

Even though all species of reptiles are unique, they can still be grouped together by their shared characteristics. Each class of animal can be broken down into smaller groups called orders. Animals in the same order are even more similar to one another than those in the same class. The class of reptiles has four main orders.

TORTOISES AND TURTLES

Tortoises and turtles have bony shells on their backs that are covered in horny plates called scutes. Many species hide in their shells when they sense danger.

SNAKES AND LIZARDS

Snakes are reptiles that have long, flexible bodies and no legs. Lizards have four <u>limbs</u> and a tail. Some lizards have long tongues they use to catch <u>prey</u>.

CROCODILES AND ALLIGATORS

Crocodiles and alligators are large reptiles with powerful jaws and tails. They spend most of their time in water.

TUATARAS

Tuataras have spiky scales, called spines, down the center of their backs and look similar to lizards.

SHELLS

Tortoises and turtles are the only vertebrates that have bony shells. This unique characteristic offers them protection from <u>predators</u> in a number of ways. Many species can tuck their heads and legs inside their shells to protect their soft body parts. However, there are a few species that can't hide in their shells, such as sea turtles. All tortoises and turtles have dome-shaped shells that make it particularly difficult for predators to crush them in their jaws.

dome-shaped shell

Shells can also help <u>camouflage</u> turtles and tortoises as their dark green colors allow them to blend in with their surroundings.

SCALES

A reptile's skin is covered in scales that help protect its body. A reptile's scaly skin helps it keep water inside its body, which means many species of reptiles are good at surviving in hot, dry, desert habitats. Scales also act like a suit of armor to protect the animal from dirt and harmful <u>parasites</u>. A reptile's scales can break, and many reptiles are able to shed their skin and grow new scales to replace the ones they have lost.

Scales are made of **keratin**, which is the same material that fingernails are made of.

COLD-BLOODED

Reptiles are cold-blooded animals, which means their body temperature changes with the temperature of their environment. To give themselves <u>energy</u>, they warm their bodies using heat from the sun. Once warm, they have the energy to move around and find food and shelter. Being cold-blooded means that reptiles can't keep themselves warm if their environment is cold. Because of this, cold climates can be very dangerous for reptiles, which is why most reptiles live in warmer parts of the world.

When a reptile sunbathes, it's called **basking.**

GETTING AROUND

Reptiles move in many different ways. Most reptiles get around by walking or running on four legs, but other reptiles can also swim, jump, and slither!

Tortoises have four legs that carry their body and shell.

Sea turtles have large flippers that help them push through water.

Snakes slither across the ground by moving the muscles in their body. They climb trees and rocks by gripping them with the large scales on their stomach.

Lizards use four legs to walk, run, and jump. They generally use their tail for balance and to grip things, such as branches of trees.

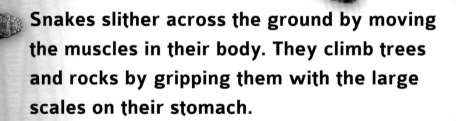

Crocodiles and alligators have four short legs they use to walk and swim.

BREATHING

All reptiles breathe using <u>organs</u> called lungs. The lungs pull in and push out air with the diaphragm, which is a muscle that sits under the rib cage. <u>Oxygen</u> enters the body through the mouth and nose, fills the lungs, and passes into the <u>bloodstream</u>. Reptiles, like all other animals, need oxygen to survive. Sea turtles are <u>aquatic</u> reptiles. This means they have adapted to live in water instead of on land. Turtles can hold their breath for between four and seven hours while underwater.

sea turtle

PREDATORS AND PREY

All animals can be sorted into groups depending on what they eat. The three groups are carnivores, herbivores, and omnivores.

herbivores
plant eaters

carnivores
meat eaters

omnivores
plant and meat eaters

Most reptiles are carnivores, which means they only eat animals, such as rodents and insects. Other reptiles, such as tortoises, are herbivores and only eat plants and fruits. There are also omnivorous reptiles, such as the box turtle, that eat things such as fish, frogs, flowers, and berries.

Animals that hunt other animals are called predators, while animals that are hunted by other animals are called prey. Crocodiles are predatory carnivores. They hunt their prey by swimming with just their eyes and ears above the water's surface.

They wait for their prey to come within reach, and then they launch toward them. They grip their prey between their strong, sharp teeth.

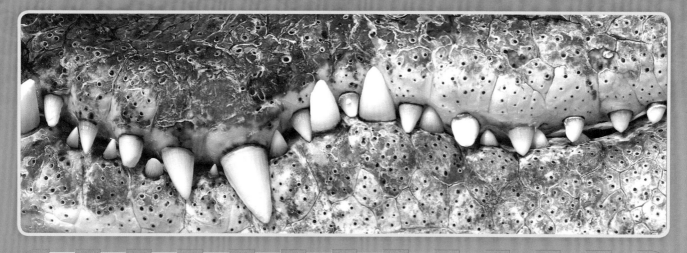

Crocodiles have powerful muscles that clamp their jaws together. The saltwater crocodile has the strongest bite of any animal.

DESERTS, RAIN FORESTS, AND SWAMPS

Habitats provide food and shelter for the animals and plants that live in them. Most reptiles live in warm habitats such as deserts and dry <u>grasslands</u>. It may seem that hardly any life can survive in the desert, but some animals and plants have learned how to survive in these extreme environments. Reptiles need very little food or water, which helps them survive in places where these things are hard to find, such as the desert. Instead, they use the sun's heat to give them the energy they need to move. <u>Tropical</u> rain forests are home to a huge variety of reptiles. The Amazon rain forest is the world's largest tropical rain forest. It provides a wide range of habitats, such as caves, swamps, and tall trees, for the animals that live there.

Deserts make up **25 percent** of all the land on Earth.

The Amazon rain forest is home to around **5 million** species of animals.

Alligators and crocodiles often live near swamps where there's a lot of mud and water. They're generally found in tropical regions of the world, such as Africa and Central America. Water helps alligators and crocodiles blend in with their environment, which makes it easier for them to take their prey by surprise. Crocodiles and alligators hunt many different types of prey. This means they're more likely to survive, as they have a wider range of prey to choose from than some other animals.

ADAPTATION

Reptiles have lived on Earth for more than 300 million years. Over time, they have adapted to their environments in many amazing ways.

Chameleons are known for being able to change color to blend in with their surroundings. This type of camouflage helps them avoid being spotted by predators. In some species of chameleons, a change in color can be used to show how they're feeling—darker colors often mean they're angry!

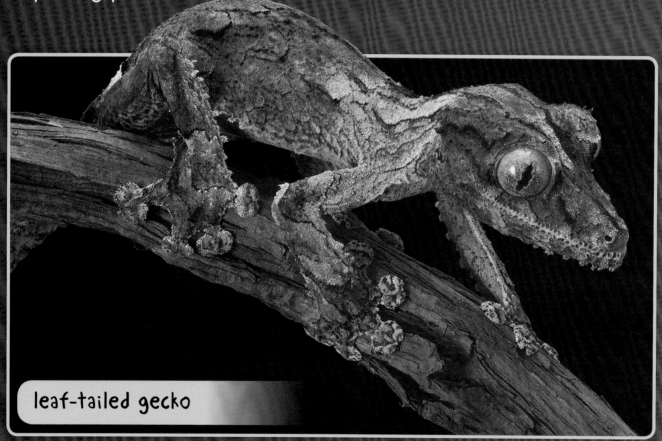

leaf-tailed gecko

Many other lizards also use camouflage to disguise themselves. The color of the leaf-tailed gecko's skin allows it to perfectly blend in with trees and leaves.

Unlike most other reptiles, turtles spend much of their lives in water, and they have adapted to survive in these habitats. Turtles have lungs, which means they come up to the water's surface to breathe. However, they can swim underwater for hours at a time without coming up for air. They're able to store a lot of oxygen in their blood and muscles. When they move their flippers, they pump oxygen into their lungs, which allows them to continue swimming without having to breathe through their mouth.

LIFE CYCLES

A life cycle is the series of changes that a living thing goes through from the start to the end of its life. Generally, reptiles start life inside soft-shelled eggs, which they eventually hatch out of. However, not all reptiles lay eggs—some species give birth to live babies that develop inside the female. Most reptiles don't look after their eggs. Instead, they bury them in the ground and leave them to hatch on their own.

Even sea turtles return to land to lay their eggs.

Unlike other reptiles, female crocodiles and alligators look after their babies. Crocodiles bury their eggs in nests by rivers and wait nearby for three months until the eggs hatch. During this time, the mother crocodile will protect its eggs from predators and other dangers. When the baby crocodiles hatch, they make a chirping noise. Their mother will dig down to the nest before carefully carrying the babies to the water's edge in her mouth. A mother crocodile will stay with its babies for a few weeks until they have grown larger and can survive on their own.

A mother crocodile can carry up to 15 babies in its mouth at one time!

egg

A Burmese python is a large snake that lives in tropical rain forests in Asia. A mother python carries its eggs inside its body for about three months before laying them. Burmese pythons can lay up to 100 eggs at a time, and they stay with their eggs for six to eight weeks. Mothers keep their eggs warm by vibrating their muscles until the eggs are ready to hatch. Once the eggs hatch, the mother leaves, and the baby pythons must survive on their own.

A Burmese python can grow more than 16.4 feet (5 m) long. At the age of four or five, the snake is ready to mate and produce more baby pythons.

reproduction

snakelet

As the young snakelets grow, their scaly skin stretches. Unlike human skin, a snake's skin reaches a point where it can't grow any bigger. When this occurs, a new layer of skin grows underneath, and as soon as it's complete, the old skin peels away. Most snakes shed their skin between two and four times every year.

adulthood

An adult Burmese python makes its home in a cave or tree and hunts other animals for food. Burmese pythons are constrictors, which means they use their strong muscles to squeeze their prey to death. They do this by biting their prey, wrapping their long body around them, and then squeezing.

EXTREME REPTILES

Some reptiles have developed extreme habits or skills that help them survive.

GIANT ANACONDA

An anaconda has a long, thick body with strong, powerful muscles. It has thick, scaly skin that's dark green, yellow, and black, which helps it blend in with trees and the ground. Anacondas often lie in shallow swamps and streams as they wait for their prey to pass. The anaconda is a constrictor, which means it wraps itself around its prey and squeezes until it dies. A record-breaking anaconda measured in at 27.7 feet (8.43 m) from head to tail. That's longer than a bus!

Anacondas don't lay eggs. They give birth to up to 80 **live** snakes at one time.

Size:
15 feet
(4.6 m) long

Home:
rain forests in South America

Diet:
fish, birds, and mammals

GALÁPAGOS GIANT TORTOISE

The Galápagos tortoise is the largest living species of tortoise on the planet. These tortoises are only found on the Galápagos Islands in the Pacific Ocean. They're extremely peaceful creatures and like to spend their days grazing on grass and leaves, as well as basking in the sun. They sleep for nearly 16 hours every day! Their huge bodies can store large amounts of water, which means they can survive for up to a year without eating or drinking.

The oldest Galápagos tortoise was **152 years old!**

Size:
4.9 feet
(1.5 m) long

Home:
Galápagos
Islands

Diet:
plants and fruits

KOMODO DRAGON

The Komodo dragon is a huge reptile that lives on Indonesian islands. Komodo dragons are the world's heaviest lizards, and they are deadly predators. They will eat almost anything they find, including deer, fish, and even humans! When a Komodo dragon spots its prey, it springs into action and uses its sharp claws to hold the animal down. A quick bite with its sharp teeth passes <u>venom</u> into its prey. The Komodo dragon does this because if the prey escapes, the venom will weaken it, and the Komodo dragon will still be able to finish its meal.

Size:
9.8 feet
(3 m) long

Home:
grasslands on
Indonesian
islands

Diet:
large and small
animals and
even humans

ALLIGATOR SNAPPING TURTLE

The alligator snapping turtle is one of the largest freshwater turtles in the world. It has a spiky shell, beak-like jaws, and a thick, scaly tail. The alligator snapping turtle spends most of its time lurking in murky waters in swamps and shallow, freshwater rivers. This turtle has one of the most unique hunting methods of all reptiles. On the end of its tongue is a small, pink piece of skin that looks like a worm. The turtle wiggles this piece of skin in order to attract prey. Fish, frogs, and birds can all mistake this for a juicy worm and then jump straight into the turtle's mouth.

Size:
2.6 feet
(0.8 m) long

Home:
southeastern
United States

Diet:
small animals and
aquatic plants

REPTILES IN DANGER

HABITAT DESTRUCTION

According to some scientists, almost one-fifth of the world's reptile species is at risk of <u>extinction</u>. One of the biggest threats to reptiles is the disruption or destruction of their natural habitats. As the human population grows, towns and cities are built on areas of land that are important habitats for reptiles and other animals. Large areas of forests around the world have been burned down or cleared for farmland or housing. This has left many animals unable to find shelter and food, which leaves them unable to survive.

WATER POLLUTION

Human waste and <u>pollution</u> have affected animal life around the world—from the thickest jungle to the deepest ocean. The garbage in the ocean comes from many places, including garbage that is thrown into rivers and then flows into the sea. Once in the ocean, the garbage can last for years, which creates a great danger for the animal life in the area. Sea turtles all over the world often get caught in garbage in the ocean and many of these turtles eventually die. It's extremely important that we never throw garbage on the ground or into water so we don't put animals in danger.

FIND OUT MORE

BOOKS

Everything Reptiles
by B.A. Hoena and Brady Barr
(National Geographic, 2016)

Reptiles
by Grace Jones
(BookLife, 2017)

WEBSITES

BBC NATURE
www.bbc.co.uk/nature/life/reptile
Discover all the different species of reptiles and their habitats.

San Diego Zoo Kids
kids.sandiegozoo.org/animals/reptiles
The San Diego Zoo's reptile page features pictures of and facts about many amazing reptiles.

GLOSSARY

adapted	changed over time to suit an environment
aquatic	living in or near water
bloodstream	the blood that circulates around the body
camouflage	the use of colors, shapes, or patterns to help an animal hide in its environment
energy	power to do a job
extinction	the process of a species dying out
grasslands	large areas of dry land covered in grass
limbs	arms, legs, and wings
organs	the parts of animals that have specific, important jobs
oxygen	a gas all animals need to survive
parasites	living things that survive by feeding off of live animals or plants
pollution	the act of adding harmful things to the environment
predator	an animal that hunts other animals for food
prey	animals that are hunted by other animals
reproduction	the process by which living things create more living things
species	a group of very similar animals that are capable of producing babies together
tropical	referring to warm and wet areas near the equator
unique	unlike anything else
venom	a poison produced by some animals
vertebrate	an animal with a backbone

INDEX